The Heart-Broke Hamster Workbook

Volume Five of The Sit 'N' Do Nothing Hamster Series

Humans **A**ll **M**ake **S**ome **T**ime **E**xploring **R**elationships

Written By Wendy Proteau

Covers designed by: Wendy Proteau

The Heart-broke Hamster

I'm so sorry you're going through something tough. I want you to know you are not alone. Many people are going through the exact same thing. Break-ups, divorce, separation, it's not easy. Even harder, is losing someone suddenly or from illness. However it happened you have to learn to be without a wife, husband, girlfriend, boyfriend, friend or partner.

For some it comes suddenly and without warning. While others, it's been a slow break down over time. Some make the choice to end things because it just wasn't working anymore. Some are mutual decisions. No matter what the reason, it leaves a space in our lives until we slowly begin to move forward.

There are no right words to make any of this easier. No amounts of "I'm sorry to hear" will make up for what you feel. It's just how life is–hard at times. Even when we choose this outcome it has an effect on the inside. We may say "I am way better off" or "I'm happy about it all"...yet, it leaves that corner in our heart that needs mending.

This book was written from going through such moments and watching those I care for having heart-wrenching circumstances to face. I tried to think of every possible thing to help you through and it may seem silly to write your thoughts down, but perhaps it will give you some clarity in this cloud.

Maybe it's time to stop and just reflect on the big picture. I bet you're doing what needs to be done, but I'm thinking you could use some time to just look at it all in the quiet moments.

Seems no matter what you do in life we all have our share of these moments. Rich or poor, it is the one common thread we all share–loss, pain, grief and hurt.

You have this book from a friend, family member, best friend, buddy or neighbor who's reaching out to you. Maybe you've picked it up on your own to just look at things. No matter how you got it, someone wants to see how you're doing with it all and make sure you'll be okay.

These are straightforward questions that we often don't share at this time. Many things we get frustrated by and we have a hard time to see the future, but it will come when we're ready.

You are an accumulation of every moment you've experienced. You've lived, loved, helped, cared and probably touched more lives than you thought. This probably isn't the first hurt and I'm sure it won't be the last. Nothing is ever easy. Maybe learning how to open up about it all might help us to reach out to one another in tough times.

Everyone in this world feels pain and sorrow. We've all loved and lost at one time or another. There is no right or wrong way of doing things. You're in the here and now of what you feel and I have no doubt you'll find your way. You're strong, smart and so much more than what you are going through at this moment, even if you can't see it all too clearly right now.

With the world moving so fast with internet, text, bills, responsibilities, work, obligations, emails…we are ever in search of what works in our life. So let's just stop and sit n do nothing for a moment but focus on you. So grab a pencil, you may want to change answers here and there as you go through it. Just one rule…

"GOTTA BE HONEST!"

I hope this helps in finding your way. Just take some time for you!
Big Big Hugs!

The Heart-broke Hamster Basics

Reflections of _______________and what I feel
(First name please)

Today's date is:_______________

Last name______________________________

I live in _______________________________

Born ______ day _________ month _______ year

Born in __________________________________

Time I was born was at______________________

Raised in________________________________

Other places I've lived over the years:

____

____

____

Education level is ________________________

I went to the following schools-name and year please:

____

____

____

I work as a______________________________

I have been at my current job ________years

I have worked in my trade _____ years

I am going through one of the following-(please circle the appropriate answer):

Break-up Divorce Separation Grieving my partner

This book was given to me by______________________________

In 5 words I would describe who I am as

1__________________________________

2__________________________________

3__________________________________

4__________________________________

5__________________________________

In 5 words I would describe the person who gave me this book as

1_________________________________

2_________________________________

3_________________________________

4_________________________________

5_________________________________

See, not so hard
YOU CAN DO THIS!

The Heart Broke Hamster

Volume Five

1-Well it's a rough spot in life right now or you wouldn't have this book. It's not easy when things are amiss in our world. It sends us into a head spin if you will. Let's get a handle on it.

You had a disagreement _______yes _______no

You've broken up with a partner _______yes _______no

They've broken up with you _______yes _______no

You had a huge fight _______yes _______no

You've lost someone _______yes _______no

You're going through a separation or divorce _______yes _______no

How long have you known them _________________________ days/months/years

2-So let's see when this all started, shall we? Think back to each of the following dates with this person and on a scale from 1-10. Mark what you felt about them at each interval (1 being wonderfully happy with-10 being not so much)

Last week_____ Last month_____ 3 months ago_____ 6 months ago_____

12 months ago_____ 5 years ago_____

Well that's far enough back to get an idea of their importance in your world. For some the connection may not go back that far, while for others it could be a lifetime.

3-We all know nothing is ever smooth in life. We all have foibles, problems, losses, disagreements, etc…We wouldn't be human if everything just sailed along smoothly (would be nice though, wouldn't it?) Let's see how you've been lately. Sometimes we go through rough spots ourselves and don't even know we are acting differently.

For the past week you would describe yourself at home in two words as being:

_______________________________ _______________________________

Now at work, you've been:

______________________________ ______________________________

When you're alone, what one word would describe your thoughts in general right now:

____

4-So while we have you focused on you, what things have you done just for you? We all get busy and need to give ourselves a break once in a while. Whether watching our favorite show, reading a book or simply getting a good night's sleep for a change-what 5 things have you done for you in the past month:

1____

2____

3____

4____

5____

5-Often we don't take time to treat ourselves when we should. It seems the bills, work, problems we take care of first. Think back and answer these:

a-The last time you bought yourself something special was in which month _________

It was ____

b-The last time you did something really special for you was in which month _________.
(could be out to dinner, a friends place…anywhere really)

Did you go somewhere: _______ yes _______no

Where____

What did you do __________________________________

c-The last time you got together with a close friend was when ____________________

Did you stay in _______ or go out ________

6-At times we forget about those moments. Seems our lives are busy interacting with people we need to, instead of those we may want to. If you could see any close friend right now at your door, you'd like to see:

____

What would you need them to do when you open that door (top 3)

____________________ ____________________ ____________________

7-In times of trouble we all have our go to- people. The people we can talk to about anything, anytime. Let's name your go-to people (family and friends.) First names only and start with the top of the list of those you can tell everything to, no matter how bad, good, sad, ugly or funny:

__________________________ __________________________

__________________________ __________________________

__________________________ __________________________

We all have people who seem to be more objective. We may not know them as well as our top list, yet they seem to have keen insight. We don't often tell them every detail, just the "hey what would you think if this were to happen to you"? Name who you've turned to in the past:

__________________________ __________________________

__________________________ __________________________

__________________________ __________________________

There are people who don't turn to anyone and I wonder about how they manage. We all know someone like that-they just do his or her own thing and don't ever want an outside opinion. At times you don't even know there is something wrong. Name those types please

__________________________ __________________________

__________________________ __________________________

__________________________ __________________________

Now what about those people who constantly ask what you think, yet don't listen to a word you say. Yep it's almost like they tell you what's going on just to get a reaction. List those 'help me please and watch me not listen' people.

__________________________ __________________________

__________________________ __________________________

__________________________ __________________________

And last, we get those people who just seem to not get it at all. They are the yes people and agree with everything and never really have an opinion of their own to share or don't want to get involved-list who they would be:

__________________________ __________________________

__________________________ __________________________

__________________________ __________________________

8-Now that was easy to figure out, we all know someone who fits into most of these categories, don't we? So now that you've been able to label them all, if your friends were to do this book, where would most of them have put your name?

I am option___ or the

____

9-At times we don't quite see ourselves as clearly as our friends or family. I think it has to do with perception-when you live it, you often don't see it while others do. So, now looking from those who really do know you and from their point of view, list the 5 traits you think they'd say define you in times of trouble. This may be hard to answer, but you do know the answers. Seems when we talk to them they usually tell us outright don't they? You're being too cautious, too hard on yourself, too bull headed, too smart for this, too giving, too soft, emotional etc….

__________________ __________________ _________________

_________________ __________________

10-With that question comes the top 5 traits that get us through day to day. These are the 5 reasons why people believe in us, why we have friends or family we're close with. Those top five traits they would say I have are:

__________________ ____________________ _________________

__________________ __________________

11-We are all a make-up of such a mixture of things-good, bad, fun, sad, talents, character-we are all unique and no two people are exact. We may have similarities, but we are all individual. So I want you to rate each of these words. We all have good and bad points about ourselves so you gotta be honest. On a scale of 1-10 (#1 being I show this a lot and my friends/family have said this to me, #10 being no one I know would say that's me-and everything in between) there are more on the next page

____Fun

____Introspective

____Taker

____Spoiled

____Inventive

____Demanding

____Understanding

____Pig headed

____Heart on your sleeve

____Social butterfly

____Analytical

____Creative

____Loving

____Patient

____Hard working

____Caring

____Self-involved

____Giving

____Intelligent

____Educated

____Stubborn

____Lazy	____Social	____Compassionate
____Outgoing	____Shy	____Emotional
____Loner	____Attentive	____High maintenance
____Successful	____Moody	____Welcoming
____Selfish	____Physically active	____Funny
____Artistic	____Argumentative	____Independent
____Free spirited	____Logical	____Level headed
____Passionate	____empathetic	____self-indulgent

Well that is hard to admit a lot of those-no one is perfect, yet we are perfectly us. We will come back to this later…trust me.

12-Whew, let's take a break from the hard stuff. We have so many other things going through our heads right now and I guess you'll figure out what to do about it all. In general, how do you handle life's troubles? Some may have a few steps in doing so, so letter them A,B,C,D, etc… in order of how you handle things normally. Not all will apply, everyone's different-So I:

1-Tackle them head on-confront it______	2-Wait it out to see what happens______
3-Ask around for advice______	4-Tend to avoid dealing with them______
5-Shy away from saying what I feel____	6-Question from all angles first_____
7-Find quickest resolutions always_____	8-Listen openly to the other person_____
9-Am right always_____	10-Back down to keep the peace_____

11-Wait till they approach_____

When we deal with others, it is hard to keep focused on the here and now, especially when things happen repeatedly. I mean some people just know how to push our buttons and they do-sometimes unintentionally, sometimes yep-deliberately. I guess it's all in our reaction-If we don't show that it affects us they no longer have the button.

So let's ask this, would you consider your buttons: (Easily pushed, hard to get to, etc…)?

____

13-Well I wonder how you normally handle things. Do you tend to keep doing the same things over and over? For as often as someone upsets us-we've done things to upset others. Doesn't matter if its friends, family or work colleagues, it seems when we go to our friends and talk about what's going on they have phrases they use. Have friends ever said:

You always do this ________yes ______no

Here we go again ________yes ______no

You have to stop ________yes ______no

You have a habit of ________yes ______no

Those are the phrases you hear, but if you hear them frequently from folks, yep…we got a pattern and we didn't even know it.

14-We often learn how to deal with things by watching others: whether parents, friends or partners-we sometimes follow the way they do things in life. It's hard to really put a finger on just where we picked stuff up, but you would say you deal with things much the same as?

who__________________________________

15-This life is all about getting through to the next day, it's never easy and it's a lot of hard work. I often wish there was a book we could reference like 'the what do to if this happens book', but of course no such book exists. There are many books out there about helping ourselves or giving us new perspectives and I've read a few of them. Some I liked, some not so much, but I did read them.

Have you ever read them _______yes _______no

How many have you read _______

Did you get a better understanding of life _______yes ______no

Did you put into practice things you read _______yes _______no

Which one was your favorite ____

Is there one you'd like to read now ____

16-We all go to school to learn the basics in life, Math, English, Geography…and I often think there should have been courses available at a young age for life's struggles. Imagine taking the 'how to play nice with others always' or 'how to deal with loss' course. It would've made life a lot easier for some things. Think about what you know right now in life. What 3 courses do you wish they would've had in school for dealing with life's troubles

____

____

____

17-Wonder if the world would be easier with a few of those under our belt? We're all individuals and we all have pet peeves, the things that others do that just make us crazy. And in troubled times, yep they're magnified, aren't they?

So let's find out all about what bothers you the most. On a scale from 1-10, mark the things that just get to you more now (#1 being that's the most annoying-#10 being you don't notice)–these are just a few, we'll do more later

____People who interrupt

____People moving your things

____Untidy dressing

____Rude behavior

____Forgetfulness

____Helplessness

____Meticulous people

____Crude manners

____Lights left on for no reason

____Untidy home

____Know it all people

____Forgetting to call if late

____Laziness

____Inconsideration

____People who brag

____Arrogance

18-It seems when we're down, a lot of little things bother us that normally wouldn't (Just how it goes.) But no matter what you're going through right now-you still have a lot of good things around you, we just at times forget to see them-(kinda tunnel vision). Yep, seems when we're troubled we focus on the bad, so let's get a wider view shall we. I want you to think about all the good things about your life and rate all the ones that apply to you. Now we aren't gonna go through all life's things, but we'll start with these:

A=good B=not bad C=can do better D=will work on it. (You notice there is no F for failure everything is achievable on here) These are all pretty much external things you have that you may not have stopped to think about:

A job that makes money	______
Family who care about me	______
A roof over my head every night	______
Food everyday-I'm not starving	______
At least one best friend	______
Many friends I appreciate	______
Accomplished many things in this life	______
Kids who love me	______
Neighbors I talk to	______
Little things that make me happy-music, TV, furniture	______
A way to get around-vehicle/bus	______
A pet that adores me	______
Hobbies I enjoy	______

I'm sure you've thought of a few more while choosing these, so fill in at least 4 more things you own or physically have around you that make you happy:

____________________________ ____________________________

____________________________ ____________________________

19-Along with that list, you know who you are and I'm sure you have many characteristics you're darn proud of! For me, I'm glad I'm stubborn, honest and funny to name a few. They've gotten me through some of the toughest moments of my life, no matter what hurts I went through. So list the top 5 things you are so proud that you are:

_______________________ _______________________ _______________________

_______________________ _______________________

20- I'm hoping by now you're starting to feel better. I know the hurts aren't easy and we all go through them. Whether we pick the wrong people to love at the time, a friend makes us angry or we lose someone. We're all just looking for what works in life and we have to go through a lot to get there. Nothing is ever easy or fair. Looking over your entire history of other people in your life, let's see how you're doing so far.

In total, I have been in # _______ serious relationships

The longest relationships I've had are (top 3)

_________months/years _________months/years _________months/years

Now the friend list:

In total I have had #________best friends in life so far.

The longest friendships have been (top 3)

_________months/years _________months/years _________months/years

21-Looking backwards is always easy. We can see what we've learned from each person long after we've moved on. Some relationships we still don't understand why we were with them-kinda the what was I thinking feeling. Some helped us become who we are supposed to be, teaching us what we need and want in life. It seems with each connection it's a learning process.

So let's see what you've learned from each of the top 3 from your lists. These 3 stood out in your life for a reason and you spent a lot of time with them. At the time it was hard to be objective-but there were both good and bad about being around them. We're going to do both sides of the coin here (gotta take the good with the bad) For each on your list, state in one sentence what one positive thing you learned about being with each of them:

Top 3 Relationships people:

1____

2____

3____

Top 3 Best Friends:

1____

2____

3____

Now fill in the one thing that wasn't so good or the hardest lesson you learned about being with each of them:

Top 3 Relationships person:

1____

2____

3____

Top 3 Best Friend:

1____

2____

3____

When you look at things at a distance it makes more sense. We all go through things in order to get to the next steps in life. So now that you've had a chance to reflect on the past, think about who you are overall.

Knowing these six people helped me __________% to become who I am today.

22-That was a tough one. I guess we live and learn every day. And when you go through tough times it's easy to not see the why behind it. At times, I wish I knew back then what I know now…would have made life way easier. What is the one thing you wish you could have known way back that you know now?

____

23-So let's start looking ahead. I know it's hard to when upset or hurt to look far in advance, but tomorrow will come and we still are busy with normal everyday things-housecleaning, work…So what is the plans for:

Today____

Tomorrow____

Yep, time never stops-we still gotta do all the normal stuff. Let's find out about your routine in life right now:

You work ________ days a week

You have to pick up groceries this coming ________________(day of the week)

Laundry day is _________________

For dinner tonight you are going to have ____

You clean your house _____times a week

Usually the big cleaning day is ________________________

Seems you still straighten stuff out _______ days a week

You make sure to talk to friends at least _________ times a week/month

And you make time for family at least ___________times a week/month

You work out or get exercise ________________times a week

Yard work is usually done _____ times a week

24-Now when some people get down, they stop doing the normal things. I have friends who don't even get dressed and stay in the Pajama's all day. So I wonder are you:

Staying in your sleep clothes all day long ______yes ______no

Are you eating regular ______yes ______no

How long are you watching TV _____hours/day

Answering the phone when it rings always ______yes ______no

Spending time on the computer _____ hours/day

Brushing your hair ______yes ______no

Brushing your teeth ______yes ______no

Showering as usual ______yes ______no

Following your daily schedule ______yes ______no

What about getting enough rest? Are you making sure to at least try to get sleep every night or are you sleeping far too much lately?

How much sleep you getting every night ______ hours

How many hours are you focusing on this other person ______/day

I know for some people it's like water off a duck's back and they continue on as normal, positive and focused on the chores at hand.

In your opinion, you would say you are dealing with this all:

_____very well _____ working on it _____struggling ____not so good

25-We've all been through something tough, it's really what we all share in common worldwide. We've probably helped many others through the rough spots in life, so think back on all the people you've known who have gone through troubles, break ups and hurts

Who was it that had the worst time getting past it: _____________________

Who seemed to handle it all the best: ______________________

26-If you look at society with all the separations, divorces, break ups…it's almost the norm. The percentages aren't great for successful long-term relationships. I wonder why? Let's take an objective look. Grade each of the following (A-D) that you believe plays a factor in most of today's relationship breakdowns:

Now these are overall in society-not your situation.

A=huge factor, B=somewhat, C=very little, D=doesn't play a role

____Too much time working

____Lack of trying

____Wanting too much too fast

____Jumping in too soon to permanent

____Sexual intimacy too fast

____Impatience

____Shallow ideals-putting looks 1st

____Not understanding what we want

____Not looking at the big picture

____Money issues

____Taking, not giving enough

____Being dishonest-hiding the truth

____Not being compatible to start with

____Not happy with who we are individually

____Too materialistic

____Settling for wrong person

____Lack of communication

____Giving up is just easier

____Addictions

____Not dating long enough

____Lack of understanding

____Competing with others

____Placing blame on the other person

____Lack of will to try

____Focus on individual needs too much

____Expecting too much from others

____Infidelity/cheating

____Not taking responsibility

____Attracted to wrong type of person

____Not holding people accountable

____Expecting partner to change

____Social standing

I don't know why things go wrong. Seems years ago people stayed together longer, not that it was always the best relationship, but they invested time because things weren't so easy back then.

27-I wonder what it would have been like to live back then. Way back when family arranged marriages. At times it was for alliance of families and others it was the best match. Often you didn't know your spouse before the wedding. Divorce wasn't common, so you stuck it out no matter what. Wouldn't be easy, but it was what it was and you had to accept it all.

Would/could you, trust your parent/parents to pick a partner for you ____yes ____no

If not a parent, but you had to trust one person to pick out a partner for your life, you'd let

______________________________ do the picking.

Could you make an arranged marriage work ____yes ______no

Learn to love someone you never met before ____yes ______no

Learn to work side by side day and night _____yes _____no

Have the patience to adapt to this partner _____ yes _____no

Put wishes aside for what was expected of you _____yes _____no

That's a little hard to fathom in this day and age, but back then it was normal life. You set out in the world and built from ground up everything you had. Your nearest family member could be 1000 miles away and neighbors/friends miles away. They didn't have phones or instant communication like we do. When you think of it, often men were called away to war for months or years at a time. Even hunting for food was often a long excursion. Letters took months to get to destinations, so how did they manage it all? In today's society we panic if we don't get that phone call every day so I wonder how you'd do. On a scale from 1-10 (1 being easy, 10 being no way) rate each of the following:

Go months waiting for communication from family _____ yes _____ no

Handle things all alone when partner is away _____ yes _____ no

Build everything just you and your partner (home, barn) _____ yes _____ no

Keep yourself entertained-no social life at all _____ yes _____ no

Raise many children with little provisions _____ yes _____ no

Writing was the only way to keep in touch _____ yes _____ no

That's just crazy isn't it, we have everything so convenient and handy. We're a button away from talking to someone and a short drive we have all we need at our fingertips.

28-Let's focus on your current situation and go through all the feelings running through your head. You've thought a lot about this, you've maybe cried, are angry, hurt, a whole barrage of emotions I'm sure. So let's answer these. Now I want you to target the exact thing and answer in 1 sentence only, no ranting…just the first thing that comes to mind. Ready? Here we go:

What is the one thing you are most angry about

____

What is the hardest thing for you to accept

____

What is the one thing you would like to say to that person

____

What is your biggest fear about it all

____

What have you learned about yourself from this all

____

What one trait/characteristic will you make sure to watch for in the next person

____

29-Did it feel good to get some of that out of your head? I know when I'm upset I think it over then talk to people who know me best. I 'm not one for confrontation, so I sit and write a letter and re-write it over and over until it says what I need to say. That way I get it all sorted out in my head. Now it depends on the situation, if I'm upset it'll be short, if I'm downright hurt it's a 10-20 pager, and at times I send it to the person, at others, I use it just to work through it all. It's about cleansing things out of my head, so it's not really about the other person. So let's ask:
What helps you to get to the heart of the matter so you can see it clearly? Do you:

Write it out _______ yes ______ no

Vent to friends _______ yes ______ no

Mull it over in your head _______ yes ______ no

React first-think later _______ yes ______ no

Pull away from the world _______ yes ______ no

Try to see all sides _______ yes ______ no

Confront the other person _______ yes ______ no

Turn to things to numb it all _______ yes ______ no

Prefer not to analyze it all _______ yes ______ no

Seek professional advice _______ yes ______ no

Let time take care of it _______ yes ______ no

We all have our own ways. For some it's straightforward to the point and others, it's a process.

30-They say things get easier with time; man they have a lot of sayings that are meant to make us understand why we hurt, don't they? On a scale from 1-10 how you feel about some of those sayings. (1 being absolutely true, 10 being yeah right)

Time heals all wounds ______

No use crying over spilt milk ______

What goes around comes around ______

People get what they deserve ______

Live and learn ______

I'd rather love and lose than never love at all ______

What is meant to be, will be ______

Everything happens for a reason ______

Where god closes a door, he opens a window ______

That's just a few, but sometimes when you're down, don't ya want to just poke the person in the eye when they say it? They mean well so maybe there is something to those sayings.

31-Thinking back over your lifetime, I'm sure you've had many people come into your life and you went through many hurts. Looking back, let's see if the past troubles did in fact follow any of those sayings…Did/Are:

Time heal the wounds eventually ___ yes ___ no

Your previous hurts teach you about things ___ yes ___ no

Those from your past go through hard times after you ___ yes ___ no

You glad you cared for others in the past ___ yes ___ no

God bring new people to your life afterwards ___ yes ___ no

Previous hurts turn out ok-it was meant to be ___ yes ___ no

They worth all the tears looking back ___ yes ___ no

32-You ever notice when you're going through something it seems like the radio DJ's know it? They play every heart wrenching song on the darn radio and I think they're in on it together, because you switch stations and poof, there's another one. I know many a time I had to pull over because I couldn't see out the window for the tears. You're laughing, but you know what I'm talking about. So what songs are they for you, lately? Yep, name them:

1____

2____

3____

4____

5____

I know when I'm sad or hurting; at times I sit at home and play the songs deliberately on the stereo. I like to reflect on it all, it somehow helps me get through in a weird, warped sort of way.

33-At times it reminds us of a particular person or moment. You do it too-don't fib! So, if you have been deliberately putting on any songs right now to just reflect-Name the top 5:

1______________________________________

2______________________________________

3______________________________________

4______________________________________

5______________________________________

34-My sister would be laughing about all this because she knows me so well and I know she's gonna kick my butt out of the doldrums. It's funny how people close to you just give you that extra push to get back in the game. Who is your boot in the butt person?

____

35-As tough as life is right now, you know that you need to move forward and it goes in stages for most people. There's hurt, denial, anger, then acceptance and change (when we re-empower ourselves.) At times we can relate to the songs that give us that encouragement to get on with life. For me, those songs just encouraged me to move on and I still get that little rush of yep 'I'm okay' when I hear it-brings back that memory. Thinking on all your past problems, what top 5 songs gave you that "I'm OK and moving proud and in charge" feeling?

1____

2____

3____

4____

5____

I'm hoping by re-visiting those moments, you're getting that inside 'I can get past this' feeling. Means you are thinking on more positive moments in your life.

36-Since we're on the positive, let's look at what you'd like to do for yourself in the future. I know when I hit a rough spot I like to treat myself to something special. It gives me that little spur of I'm on my way. Will you treat yourself to any of the following?

New clothes/outfit ______ yes _____ no

Vacation somewhere ______ yes _____ no

Spa day ______ yes _____ no

Hair style ______ yes _____ no

Massage ______ yes _____ no

Dinner out ______ yes _____ no

Favorite dessert ______ yes _____ no

Sexy clothing ______ yes _____ no

Night out with friends ______ yes _____ no

Hot steamy candlelight bath ______ yes _____ no

Is there one thing you'd like to just buy for yourself? Whether that movie, computer, TV, Gym membership…something you just feel would recharge you-be realistic:

You'd like to buy ____

37-At times when we go through stuff, it gives us the opportunity to re-invent who we are. I mean no sense in just looking at all the negative stuff. The growing pains allow us to reflect and move forward with new ideas. We both know you've been thinking a lot about it all. Now these are all first response-quick answers. Don't sit and ponder it or think too hard-just fill in the blanks with the first positive thoughts that come to mind.

A-I really want to learn how to be more:

____

B-I think I deserve someone who is more:

____

C-I can do ________________and ___________________ to make myself happier.

D-I will always make time now for me to just

____

E-I want to try something new like

____

F-I am going to be more adventurous and

____

G-I am stepping outside my comfort zone and going to wear something like

____

I hope you're seeing this as a whole new set of possibilities for you.

38-We only get one go around at this life and at times it takes a life-altering situation for us to stop and think about it all. Some lose someone they love and don't get a second chance to say the things they wanted to. We hope they knew exactly what knowing them meant to us and that we showed them exactly how we felt every day. If you've experienced this, you know you'd give your right arm to have one more moment to express what you feel.

If you could say 3 things to a person you lost, it would be:

____

____

____

That was a question so personal you may not have even filled it in, but your thoughts went there and you probably silently answered them. It's important to think of those things and I believe the person knows it or can see what you're going through. It also helps people realize to not forget the little things in life every day like kindness, caring, patience, understanding, times we never get a 2nd chance.

39-As tough as that was it may help us to see who we are in this lifetime. I'm sure we all hope to be remembered fondly when our time comes, but do we really strive to reach that mark? We all like to think we're doing okay.

I live the way I hope people will always remember me as ________% of the time

I try to show kindness at least ______% of the time

I make sure to be there for others _______% of the time

I tell people I care about them and they're important to me _____% of the time

I have done a random act of kindness ______ times

I try to understand others and be empathetic at least _______% of the time

I show compassion ______% of the time

I try to focus on others and those in my life _______% of the time

40-I wonder with answering those questions does it spur you on to think differently and perhaps step back for a moment and re-think what you feel right now? I've always said to picture the person you're angry with in a coffin. How would you remember them? In question 11, I asked you to put on a scale from 1-10 of all your good and bad points. (1 being it's totally you and everyone who knows you would agree, and 10 not you at all) So thinking of the person that just left your life, (now that you've had time to think about everything and work through some of this) let's fill this in again for that person. Be fair, it is hard to put the hurt and anger aside, but I need you to be objective.

If they were gone from the face of the earth tomorrow…you'd say that person was:

Fun	______	Pig headed	______
Hard working	______	Introspective	______
Heart on my sleeve	______	Caring	______
Taker	______	Social butterfly	______
Self-involved	______	Spoiled	______
Giving	______	Inventive	______
Creative	______	Intelligent	______
Demanding	______	Loving	______
Educated	______	Understanding	______
Impatient	______	Stubborn	______
Lazy	______	Active socially	______
Compassionate	______	Outgoing	______
Shy	______	Open	______
Loner	______	Attentive	______
High maintenance	______	Successful	______
Moody	______	Welcoming	______
Selfish	______	Physically active	______
Funny	______	Artistic	______
Level headed	______	Passionate	______
Patient	______	Analytical	______

Told you we would come back to this. Now I'm sure you're still not happy with what you're going through. That person has flaws, good points, just like you do and sometimes in the big picture we forget that they are just people who make mistakes, do bonehead things and hurt as well. If you look back, sometimes the reasons things happen are revealed years down the road.

41- We cross paths with many people in life and it's funny how we feel an inner voice guide us. Have you ever been in a room full of people and you just get an uneasy feeling about one in particular? They don't look any different or act any different…we just don't get a sense of ease with them. Just as the people we bring close to our lives, we follow that inner voice somehow. Tis amazing when you think about it-we have radar!

Do you hear/feel that voice inside _____yes _____no

You have listened to that voice _____% of the time

You have ignored it when you knew better ______% of the time

42-Now that your life is in this moment, you must be somewhat curious about what is coming around the bend. No matter what happens, the future holds many mysteries. What are your wishes for what lies ahead? At times we have to make changes for the future. Just answer yes or no

In the next 3 months I can see myself:

Getting out and doing things I enjoy _______

Making time to spend with friends _______

Taking some extra time to enjoy a hobby _______

Taking more time to play sports _______

Chatting more with people _______

Learning to socialize more: going to dinner _______

Going dancing _______

Attending social functions _______

Entertaining at your place _______

Joining a date site for meeting people _______

43-The computer has paved the way for people to communicate all over the world. It gives us the chance to step out and talk with people in other places. It doesn't matter if it's across the city or across the globe, people are basically all the same and at times it's wonderful to learn about others. Thru work you may talk to people from everywhere. I don't know what you do for a living, so let's ask questions on the work side first.

Where is the furthest point you contact through work ______________________________

Is there anyone in particular that you look forward to seeing the email from

____

Who is the person you can joke with the most _____________________________________

Who seems to be the biggest complainer ____

Who is the most demanding one ____

If you could meet just one person you talk to who would it be

____

Who is the flirtiest one ____

44-Now the world of the home computer

Do you chat on the computer a lot _______ yes ______ no

Do you belong to any sites _______ yes ______ no

What is your favorite site ____

How many people have you gotten to know really well _______

You contact each other at least _______ per day/week/month

Do you ever use the date sites they have now _______ yes ______no

If so, which have you had the most luck with ___________________________________

How many lifelong friends do you feel you have from chatting ______.

45-We're going to delve a bit into the date sites here since it seems it's the new way to meet people. If you've experienced them:

On average, you feel ______%, are truthful in how they present themselves on a profile

In general you feel ______%, are players or scam artists

You are truthful about yourself ______%, of the time

You are always sure to post updated pictures ______ yes _____no

There are a lot who don't post a picture, don't know why that is. The experts do warn about privacy and all so you feel if someone doesn't post a picture, it means they are:

_____shy _____ unsure____ insecure _____ cautious _____committed

46-There are those who are married/committed and playing on the Net. I guess it's the easy way for some to live in a fantasy world. Some reach out because they're unhappy or unfulfilled. So do you:

Personally know people who do this _____yes ______no

Think their spouse knows _____yes ______no

Think their spouse should know _____yes ______no

You feel that this is:

Ok, as long as they never act on it ______yes _____no

Harmless fantasy ______ yes ____ no

Dangerous ______ yes ____ no

A form of cheating ______ yes ____ no

A sign they should change their situation ______ yes ____ no

A way for them to escape and stay committed ______ yes ____ no

Have you ever done the same thing ______ yes ____ no

That's a tough question and it's hard for some to really understand why this happens. I brought it up in case you've experience a hurt because of it. You have to be cautious when meeting this way and protect yourself always. Never fall for someone to fast, wait until they've stepped up and proven who they are.

47-It's not easy figuring out what is true and what is false when it comes to talking on a site. You see a picture and talk for a while then decide whether to meet. They say always be smart, be safe, cautious and investigate things first. The things they always promote are meeting in a crowded public place, don't give out information such as home phone number, address until you've built trust. So, let's ask how you would handle this all. If you met someone who catches your eye on the Net

You talk online first for _____-days/weeks/months

You always give them your untraceable cell number _____ yes ____ no

You change to talking on phone after _____ days/weeks/months

Do you block your number at first when you call _____yes _____no

Provide home phone number usually after _____days/weeks/months-Or-only after you've met and are comfortable _____

You usually meet them after how long ____________________

Where do you normally meet _____________________________

Do you use the Net to investigate them first ______ yes _______no

Do you ever on the first meeting:

Let them come pick you up______ yes ______ no

Go pick them up______ yes ______ no

Meet in a private place______ yes ______ no

Do you invite them to your home______ yes ______ no

I hope you always remember safety first and protect yourself always. A genuine, interested person will understand caution and be willing to allow you to gain a sense of safety. NEVER FORGET THAT! If you answered yes to any of the last 4, please think twice and change that.

48-It's surprising the number of people connecting across the globe. I know of people who lived in different countries and are now happily married. With my luck, my perfect match is at the South Pole (brrrr)-but my hope is he is living on a beach someplace like Hawaii. It's hard to imagine picking up and moving to another country, but people do it. We can all dream, so, if you could envision your perfect partner…you are hoping they live where in the world? Now have some fun with this, could be any country

You would love to end up living in____

49-Oh it's fun to imagine things! There have been many things I've often thought about how it would be to meet that one right person. We sure go through a lot of wrong people beforehand that you really have to ask yourself, would I recognize my perfect partner?

Let's figure out what you really think you want for your next relationship. We will start with physical appearance first. Looking back over time, you have always been attracted to:

Height between _________and__________
Physique usually: (brief
description)____

____

Hair color the majority of time was __________________

Type of work they did-now you may have a few here that are similar but just mark how many for each category:

________ Office worker ________ Blue collar (factory, truck driver)

________ Management ________ Self-employed

________ Artistic ________ Tradesman (plumber/electrician)

________ Scientific fields ________ Teacher

________ Not working ________ Government job

Any to add ______________________ ___________________ ___________________

Describe in 5 words their usual top personality traits:

________________ ________________ _________________

_________________ ________________

50-Now the type of person may vary, but they are usually one or the other. In general, looking over the past, pick the one on each line that most describes your partners-you can put an initial by each line if that helps you figure out each of their traits. Go through each relationship one at a time and we'll see if you date the same type of person usually.

Introvert_____ Extrovert ______

Givers_____ Takers______

Outgoing _____ Shy ______

Steadily employed _____ Works here n there _____

Goal oriented ______ Day to day ______

Driven ______ Laid back ______

High maintenance _____ Independent _______

Loud and boisterous _____ Soft spoken _______

Motivated _______ Unmotivated _______

Hard working ______ Lazy ________

Charming _______ Tell it like it is ________

Honest and open _______ A lot of hidden things _______

Reliable _______ Unreliable ________

Responsible ________ Doesn't follow through _______

51-Is this helping you? I know I've made mistakes by picking the same type over and over and so have many of my friends-both women and men.

Would you be willing to date totally opposite to the type you normally date _____yes ____no

What about without that first spark/chemistry feeling _____yes ____no

Someone not quite what you normally physically appreciate _____yes ____no

Someone you can develop the friendship first _____yes ____no

Let's do this again now…and just fill in the blanks of what you'd be willing to try new:

Height could be between _________and__________

Physique would be ok if: (brief description)____

I'm willing to try to date people in the following fields:

________ Office worker________ Blue collar ________ Management _______Teacher

________ Self-employed________ Artistic ________ Tradesman ________ Scientific fields

Some traits I will stick with no matter what because that's just what I love.-I would be willing to try some new ideas, but I still want someone with these 3 top attributes

__________________________ __________________________ __________________________

52-I wonder if we were to slow down the process, really get to know the person beforehand and take our time deciding whether they are for us or not…would it work? How do you normally do things? Let's say you meet someone new, just ran into him or her somewhere. They seem interested, numbers are exchanged...how patient are you when it comes to:

You'd want to begin talking within ______days

If you don't hear from them you call after ______days

You'd expect them to go out with you out within _____days

You expect them call at least _____days a week

You expect them to be intimate within ______dates (how many)

You expect flowers from them within ______days/weeks

You will send flowers within _______days/weeks

You expect them to open up about their past within ______days

With changing times, I wonder how your parents would have answered those questions-or grandparents for that matter.

53-Let's say you call and leave a message but you don't hear back from them for two weeks.

You would think that means:

____

They call back eventually and tell you work has kept them busy and stuff came up around home, they just couldn't make time to call and are very apologetic

Would you still go out with them if asked _______yes _____no

How interested would you still feel _______%

Would you wait to see if they call again first ____yes _____no

Does your guard go up automatically ____yes _____no

54-People meeting people…it's never as easy as it seems, yet they have these new shows on TV where they set up one person with 25 single available people. They only know each other 3 months and big decisions are made. Seems almost ideal in the TV world, but for me I'd need way longer before I decide to commit to someone. What about you?

You feel exclusive with someone after _____dates

You discuss your expectations with the person after _____dates

You would consider moving in or marriage after _____ weeks/months/years

OR

You're not into exclusive usually _____yes _____no

You prefer to never marry _____yes _____no

55-When you meet someone, you usually take some time to get to know them and then you start introducing them to your family and friends. How long after you meet someone do you like to:

Introduce them to your best friends _______days/weeks/months

Introduce them to co-workers ______days/weeks/months

Introduce them to brothers/sisters _______days/weeks/months

Introduce them to the parents _______days/weeks/months

Introduce them to your children _______days/weeks/months

Take them to a family-wedding etc… _______days/weeks/months

Out of all the friends you have the opinion you rely on most of your new partner is:

Male friend__________________ female friend__________________

Same question for brothers or sisters-whose opinion do you trust most often after they meet them:

Brother ______________ Sister __________________

Now, the parents, you hope they impress which one the most

Mom____ Dad _____ Which one will usually sit and tell you openly what they see ______

56-At times when it doesn't all turn out like we wished, we often talk to those same people and they say stuff like-I told you I didn't like this or that. Seems at times they may have mentioned something and we just didn't listen to them, did we? Those I told you so people. Do you remember anyone saying something along those lines with regards to your current situation?

______________________________ had said

____

______________________________ had said

____

Sometimes we're lucky and they really said nothing.

57-Either way it's never easy to start over, but in time this too will fall into memory and will make sense eventually. What if every person you met in life gets you to where you're supposed to be? Sounds poetic, doesn't it? If you are meant to go through this all, this maybe forces you on a new path in life. All it takes is trying something different or seeing something in a new way to get to the future that's waiting for you? Some things you'll keep doing because it's part of who you are, but maybe you can try a couple different things. These things will never change so you'll keep doing (2 things)

____

____

But, you also want to change and start (2 things)

____

____

If you can do just a couple things differently for the next while, you're already on your way. Silly things, like going to that bookstore and spending an hour reading, or going for a 15-minute walk every day.

58-In this world it's not easy to see things at times. We get so busy with work, schedules, dealing with everyday stuff that we kinda get lost in the shuffle of habit. What if we were to try to alter the little things, doing something we don't normally do?

Do you usually smile when walking down the street or shopping _____yes ______no

Do you make small talk with people while running errands _____yes ______no

Have you stopped at that little restaurant down the street for dinner _____yes ______no

Have you gone to an art gallery lately _____yes ______no

What about going out to see a live band _____yes ______no

Volunteering in the community _____yes ______no

Going for lunch with someone at work for a change _____yes ______no

Getting in touch with relatives or friends you haven't seen _____yes ______no

59-The world is filled with things to try. Ever really thought about maybe delving into new things? If we keep doing the same things over and over, no wonder we don't experience change. So would you?

Take a dance lesson or two ____yes_____ no

Take a creative writing course just for fun ____yes_____ no

Go to a nearby festival 1 ____yes____ no

Take a painting or drawing class ____yes____ no

What about a how-to seminar ____yes____ no

60-It may not sound like fun and you're probably saying, that's just not me. Well you'll never know until you try-right? What hidden talents do you have that you've never tapped into?

Do you have any talents that you know of _______yes ________no

If yes, what are they

____

If you answered no—think again! We all have something, even if it's the gift of gab, great cook, green thumb, crafty, funny, writing, painting, drawing, singing, dancing, mechanically inclined, computer smart…Most things we haven't even tried in life because we didn't take the time.

61-Well a lot of people are now single for the first time after a long relationship. I bet it's mind-boggling! Single life has its up and downs. Depending what your situation was, you could look at this as a hardship or a blessing. I know if children are involved that is always the biggest worry-we'll get to that in a while, but there is the whole being single again thing and for everyone, it's something different.

What scares you most about being single again

____

What things are you looking forward to trying all on your own

____

Is there anything you've had to put off for so long that you're anxious to get back to

____

What is the first thing you want change about your place

____

62-Talking with friends, they felt the hardest thing about going through a break-up was the fact it wasn't forever as they planned. He thought he'd get married one time and one time only. He now can see the signals all along, but he just never really noticed them before. Some have tragically lost their partner, so this is a way to reflect about how things were over the years. In 3 words, describe what you were feeling during the relationship. What 3 words first pop into your head to describe your thoughts and how you felt for each time period

1st year was ________________ ________________ ________________

2nd year was ________________ ________________ ________________

5th year was ________________ ________________ ________________

10th year was: ________________ ________________ ________________

15th year was ________________ ________________ ________________

20th year was ________________ ________________ ________________

25th year was ________________ ________________ ________________

30th year was ________________ ________________ ________________

40th year was ________________ ________________ ________________

63-At times people marry young, they grow apart as they age or their goals and ideals change. Sometimes it's an infidelity or hardship that changes things. For others, it's the death of their partner. There are so many reasons why things change and some of them will never have an answer as to why. It takes two people to have a relationship. Sometimes it's easy to just point the finger, but sometimes it's been a series of things that just haven't gone right for a long time.

What would you say are the top 3 things that caused your relationship to end? I'm not saying it was more one person or the other-just see it objectively for a moment:

____

____

____

For some it's not losing the person, but the loss of the lifestyle that's the worst. When we're with someone, we gain a sense of comfort in having a certain way of life. Even if it wasn't the greatest, we had that other person to talk to and do things together. Even if it was a person to cook for or to argue with, there was another body we knew would be there.

Let's ask the following:

What are the three things you miss most about the lifestyle?

____

____

____

I wonder how much your social life changed. Did you keep the same friendships? At times it's hard for people around us, married friends often distance themselves feeling unsure about how to deal with the situation. We've probably done to others as well over our lifetime. It's an awkward time and you're never really sure what to say. You could be friends with both parties and just don't want to upset anyone.

Have your friends been supportive through this _______yes _____no

Is it awkward for you at times _______yes _____no

Do you socialize with them all still _______yes _____no

If you're looking back, which friends do you miss socializing with the most?
(Top 4)

__________________________ __________________________

__________________________ __________________________

64-Break ups are hard, losses even harder-we all handle them differently. But all the people you've known have played a part in making you who you are today and if you had to advertise yourself…really sell yourself

Top 3-one word answers you would describe yourself

Physically: ______________ ______________ ______________

Emotionally: ______________ ______________ ______________

Personality quirks: ______________ ______________ ______________

Scale from 1-10 now: (1 being top marks) and really be honest with who you are

____Intellectually ____Funny ____Healthy

____Smart ____Successful

____Attractive ____Charming

You are an accumulation of every moment in life till now. Look at you go!

65-We said we'd come back to the children part of things. So let's ask the following:

Do you have children from this relationship _______yes _____no

If so, how many: ________boys _______girls

I know that's your first concern. It's not easy for them to understand or go through it all, but kids are resilient and they often see things long before we adults do. I guess if they're school age, they probably talk to their friends about it all. As I said…it's almost the norm, so in school they probably learn of many other kids in the same situation. I don't know how many children you have, but you can add spaces if you have more than 6.

So what grades are your children in:

____________ _____________ _____________

____________ _____________ _____________

If they are out of school, how old are they now:

_____, _____, _____, ______, ______, _____

If this is your 2nd, 3rd or 4rth marriage, you could have a blended family with many children. Never know nowadays. If they are dealing with the loss of someone, it's hard on them too. Is there one in particular that:

Is having the most difficulty ____yes ____no

Trying to be the bravest about it all ____yes ____no

Is trying to be there more for you ____yes ____no

Is angry right now and hard to approach ____yes ____no

I wish there were the right words to say, but nothing sounds appropriate. Perhaps a professional may be able to help or family and friends can lend a hand. Even joining a group for support could help. You're in a tough spot and my heart goes out to you.

66-If it's a divorce it's tough when going through the legalities of it all. You look at all the people you know who've gone through this and watch what they've been through. It doesn't seem to work out for some and it feels like it all just doesn't make sense. Let's see how you feel about how the system works in general:

Now remember, this is looking at everyone you know….not just your situation.

The system seems to do the following-rate 1-10 (1 being absolutely is what they do, 10 not even close-and everything in between)

Looks after individuals' rights ______

Looks after the children's rights ______

Cares about the individual situation ______

Doesn't care about the final result ______

Cares about making it fair ______

Considers what's best for the child ______

Investigates thoroughly before deciding ______

Doesn't investigate enough ______

Follows the law to the T ______

Enforces what it decides ______

In general you'd say the system usually favors ____________________

In general you'd say the system works properly ______ % of the time

In a perfect world we all have an opinion on how things should go. If we could change the legal system to work for everyone, what would you wish to see happen? This is when looking at the normal relationship, I'm sure there are many with extenuating circumstances.

For example: I think it took two people to get into this situation and they should have to figure out a reasonable, fair way out of it. Both brought children into the world and both are responsible in raising them. They should each have the children half of the time, whether every second week or six months out of the year.

It would be way easier to have the children removed at the onset of a break up. They'd be out of the battles they sometimes get caught in. Force the parents to sit down with a judge who'll mediate. Children would be assessed by professionals, family and friends interviewed and all the information gathered, provided to the three parties at negotiations. The judge would look at all information provided and the couple would have to work together to settle…if they can't agree on all aspects, the outcome is what that one judge decides. Just seems way more personal for the judge to get to know both people and allow the children to have a say as well.

Possessions/debts should be 50/50 for anything accumulated after the wedding; it took the two of you to build what you had. (You can tell I'm no lawyer and a bit of a dreamer.) I just hope it would make people work things out amicably and not spending thousands on having lawyers battle things. It's not so easy in real life.

67-If you could revamp the system to work for all involved you would:

____

____

____

____

I guess in a perfect world, things would be simple, but they're not. Seems things are always complicated and if you're going through this whole process, I feel for you. I hope everything turns out workable.

68-Let's think on the more positive things right now. Your children are a legacy to who you are. They have qualities that are just like you and they make you laugh when you see those things spring up. Which of your children are most like you

In looks ____________________

In personality ________________

In humor ___________________

Which top 3 personality traits are you happy your kids have that are just like you

__________________ __________________ __________________

Which physical characteristics do they have the most from you?

__________________ __________________ __________________

I know you probably hope they do better than you at certain things in life and you may even worry they just might do the same darn things you did at times. Whether rebellious when young or too shy…which top 5 things do you hope they don't do as you did?

1____

2____

3____

4____

5____

Once you're a parent it never stops, regardless of the time you spend. Some separations get tough on the kids. They're stuck in the middle and never asked to be put there. Many people use them as bargaining chips or a way to get back at their former spouse….but, that's wrong on all accounts. If you find your time with them isn't what it used to be, have no fear, you will always be their mother or father, nothing changes that. At times their small and don't understand it all, but as they grow and learn, there will be time to rebuild. Being a parent never stops, even when your 90, you're still their parent.

69-Yep, you are who you are and it took time to get to this moment in life. Looking back over your lifespan what one thing do you still chuckle at? Like you can't believe you really did that-it was so fun and crazy:

How old were you at the time __________

What was it

____

____

70-On that same line of thinking, looking back again over every moment …what was the one thing you wish you could experience all over again from childhood? Re-live it exactly as it was:

How old were you at the time _________
What was it:

____

____

Looking back over the time with your recent partner, if you could go back and experience one moment exactly as it was:

How old were you at the time _________

What was it

____

____

71-I promised we'd ask a few more of these so we're going to do some more of what drives you nuts about other people. Like in the previous question, rate them from 1-10 (1 being-that is so annoying, 10 being couldn't care less)

Bad drivers ________

Shallow people ________

Inconsistency ________

Lame excuses ________

Road rage people ________

People who fib a lot ________

People who are late ________

Poor hygiene ________

Sloppy dressing ________

People who question (everything) ________

Non-stop talkers ________

No table manners ________

Spit when they talk ________

This is to help you vent all the crazy frustration out.

72-Well now, that was easy to figure out wasn't it? Now what are the things you just really appreciate in other people? When looking at your family and friends, people you are really close to…are there a few common traits among them? Top traits that you really enjoy in those people in your life and most possess these 6 qualities:

________________________ ________________________

________________________ ________________________

________________________ ________________________

73-Single life is not easy at first since it seems you have to learn to do a whole bunch of stuff someone else used to handle. But it can be fun! For me, I have to work, maintain a house and yard, it's hard to fit it all in. I have learned how to drywall, build, car maintenance and even a bit of electrical. Some were ok to learn and some I still don't like doing…but we gotta do it. What things do you look forward to learning how to do on your own?

______________________ ____________________

______________________ ____________________

______________________ ____________________

What things are you dreading having to do…

______________________ ____________________

______________________ ____________________

______________________ ____________________

74-I used to try to do a lot of stuff on my own then I realized some stuff is expensive if you mess it up. I often call on friends to help me out. Yep, at times they're a lifeline! Who do you think you'd call on most for some of the things you need to learn

Female would be ____________________________

Male would be ______________________________

75-It's not easy having to ask someone for help, especially when the simple things confound us. I used to think geez I should know how to do this, but I guess I never bothered to learn it through all my years. If you could go back and learn more about one thing to make your life easier right now, whether carpentry, mechanics, cooking, laundry

You would like to know more about___________________________

76-You'll find your way through it all-no worries. You know you can always depend on yourself. Being single, there are some things you should perhaps look at twice since this world has gotten tougher. The world is filled with strange people at times-so you gotta be smart about it all. When your next partner comes along, I wonder how you'll be. Will you

Believe all they tell you ______yes ______no

Ask a lot of questions _______yes ______no

Accept things at face value _______yes ______no

Test them in little ways _______yes ______no

Watch behaviors _______yes ______no

Watch for habits _______yes ______no

These are all things you have to start thinking about. In this day n age, it's not easy to tell who's upfront/ honest and who is hiding something. Tis tough out there!

77-With the world as it is, unfortunately there are those who deliberately set out to harm you. We mentioned the married people who play but there are also the people who are in it to get money or information out of you, gotta be so careful nowadays-identity theft, con artists. When first talking, it's easy to build a lot of hope on words. It's important you give the person a chance, but you really gotta be smart.

Do you make sure to get a full name________yes _______no

Do you get an address-where they live ________yes _______no

Do you make sure to let a friend or family member know:

Who you are meeting ________yes _______ no

Where you are meeting ________ yes _______no

When you are meeting ________ yes _______no

Do have them call you to check up on you during, and after ________ yes _______no

78-This may all seem like a lot of work, but once you get the details on the person-it's possible to do a full background check since you never know just who they could be. If they're honest there is nothing for them to worry about and there are many sites to get pertinent details…BE SMART! Once you get that check, don't think you are safe…still follow safety-first rules and still watch for patterns. Some people are crafty they've practiced their trade-(no matter what hard luck story they give you)

Have you experienced any of the following

Only certain times of day they call you _______yes _______no

Do they have a lot of excuses _______yes _______no

Do they make promises and not follow up _______yes _______no

Do they have a hard luck story all the time _______yes _______no

Can you reach them at anytime you choose _______yes _______no

Do you have to leave messages and they call you back _______yes _______no

Over time and once you've met several times in a public place and gained a degree of trust:

Do they avoid having you over to their home _______yes _______no

Do they make excuses for not seeing where they live _______yes _______no

Do they always want to meet in a public forum _______yes _______no

Do they tend to apologize with gifts a lot _______yes _______no

Do they seem to always tell you what you want to hear _______yes _______no

Ok, these are just a few of the things you should really think about. Being newly single, at times being lonely affects the ability to see through things so best if you always remember your life is number one priority and anyone wanting to genuinely be a part of it will understand.

79-Fun learning all this stuff, isn't it? Man…what has happened to the world? It seems with so many people playing in other's lives, the good people get lost in the shuffle. It's just sad. There are still good people out there, just by the time you've found one someone has tried to play in their world and their guard is way up. Both women and men alike have gone through troubles-it's not limited to one sex or the other. I've heard stories of what some have gone through and I can't say I blame them for being cautious and skeptical.

So if you come across a person who maybe has been hurt/played and seems a little hard to get close to, how will you handle it?

Will you
Take time to show them who you are _____ yes _____no

Not bother with them it's too hard _____ yes _____no

Allow them to check you out _____yes _____no

Let them learn at their pace _____yes _____no

Slow down your expectations _____ yes _____no

Meet several times on mutual ground _____ yes _____no

80-Seems one of the biggest problems today is people are in a rush to find someone. They take more time picking out a new car than they do a partner. It's about the here and now, they dive right in. Some even live together a few weeks/months later and then find themselves in a mess as a result, so I wonder what the hurry is? I'm sure you've seen it too. In your opinion, you believe people rush into relationships because-There may be more than one here, so just check what you feel could be contributing reasons:

They don't really care about life ____yes ____no

Lack in self-esteem ____yes ____no

It's easy ____yes ____no

Afraid of being alone ____yes ____no

Like the idea of having someone ____yes ____no

Need attention ____yes ____no

Need money ____yes ____no

Looking for someone to take care of them ____yes ____no

Can't see clearly what they want ____yes ____no

They need to feel important ____yes ____no

Are desperate ____yes ____no

Lack in common sense ____yes ____no

Need to take care of someone ____yes ____no

Have no clue what really works for them ____yes ____no

Are gullible/naive ____yes ____no

Have no inner drive to do for oneself ____yes ____no

Like the conquest-thrill of the chase ____yes ____no

Like the drama ____yes ____no

Live life with fairytale ideals ____yes ____no

Give them a false sense of security ____yes ____no

Wants children ____yes ____no

I'm sure you have checked a few of these off and if you really stand back and watch it happen to someone you know it's hard. We all know people who have done this, maybe even ourselves at one point. I may have missed some other reasons in that list, but from what you've seen you may be able to add some of your own thoughts as to why they rush in:

____

____

____

81-I hope by going through this whole book so far you've gained an understanding of what you want for yourself. No one is perfect. We all make mistakes and have foibles in life. Some big ones, some smaller, it's just how it goes. There is no right way or wrong way to do things, just lessons to learn from. Now some people are way too hard on themselves, while some aren't hard enough.

We all have the ability to strive for better-it's just hard work to love ourselves enough to follow through. So let's think about what you want.

I deserve to find real inner happiness!

(I made you read it…now say it again and again and again.)

Yep, we have to love ourselves first before anyone else can love us. That saying has been around for ages, but it's the truth. Let's work on what you think about you. If you were to look in the mirror right now-get rid of all the negative concepts (we are all our own worst critics) you can honestly say and be positive:

The eyes are our most expressive feature. They can show intelligence, heart, depth, etc…So your eyes show that you are:

____

The mouth is a wonderful thing. Lips frame the very tool we use the most-our voice and smile. The smile is the one gift we give for free always-something so simple, yet wonderful. We all like to receive one and we can give so much with that simple gesture. It can be full, sensual, defined etc… so your mouth tells the world that you are:

____

Now the hair frames the face, the experts say. Some choose to shave it off, some style it, some replace it and some are bald. But it's all a part of us, so you would say your head would state that you are:

____

Now the nose-some it's a button, some are crooked by an old break, some are distinguished, (there are so many noses) but it was placed there by divine intervention. If it weren't there, we wouldn't smell what we eat or couldn't stop to smell the roses. So some may like their nose, others not…but it's all in how you see it. Your nose is:

____

Those are only the four facial things that stand out on a person. We can be dazzled by a smile, feel all melty from a seductive glance, get lost in the feel of silky hair and enjoy the way a nose crinkles at a laugh. There are so many things that set us apart: Freckles, dimples, birthmarks, moles, lashes, coloring, brows, whiskers, moustaches-you get my drift. We are truly unique...again the snowflake thing-magically one of a kind-no two people identical. (Well except for twins I suppose, but they have differences too)

82-Now there are some people out there who just refuse to see how wonderful they truly are. Many people look at the next person and wish they looked more like them. They are never happy with themselves. The fact of the matter is, beauty is in the eye of the beholder and truly only skin-deep. We will all age and with that, we lose our youthful appearance. It's what's inside that matters, so are you going to spend your years wasting time worrying about what the outside is?

I have spent ______years worrying about my outer appearance

I have tried to change it #______ times

I want to be more like ____________________

I have beaten myself up constantly about my __________________

I worry about what others think when they see _________________

I value others' opinions ahead of mine usually ______% of the time

All those other people whose opinions I value so highly, I know them and all the details of their life and troubles:

____ really well ____somewhat ____not at all ____they are strangers

I have allowed someone to make me feel unworthy ____yes ____no

I allow people I know to criticize me ________% of the time

I allow society to tell me how I should look ______% of the time

I allow others to tell me how I should change _____% of the time.

Now you see where my questions are coming from? We at times make ourselves crazy by thinking that others' opinions count before ours. **We gotta stop that!** Only you know who you are, what you feel, what you want, what you can do and what you'll put up with. So quit putting up with it, it's time to just simply ignore those remarks and believe in who we are.

83-Now that we got that out of the way are we feeling more positive about who you are? I'm sure you've done some pretty great things in life, not that we do them every single day, but there are moments when we just helped someone out, been there for a friend, took time for family. It is those little moments that truly define who we are.

Looking back over your life span:

I have helped at least #_______ people through hard times

I have been there for at least #_______ family members

I have listened to at least #_______ tough moments for others

I have helped those I care for ______ % of the time

I have put myself aside and cared for others _____% of the time

84-If your numbers weren't as high as you'd hoped for in the questions, there is always today to start. The good thing about life is- it's never too late! Even for those really hard things we've gone through-at times, we need to forgive them inside and let them go. So many hold onto that past hurt and it keeps it alive, putting energy in its memory. Especially when most will never be resolved the way we wish. At times it is something really awful that has been done or gone through, while others it's a simple rift never resolved. You hear it all the time- forgiveness is not for the other person…it is to let it go inside of us. So let's get that out of the way. This is a tough one and it may take you time to think about it. If you need to come back to this…take your time, we are going to get rid of them all. List three people or situations:

I want to forgive: ___________________________

____

____

Check off the following when you truly believe you're ready. I don't want to waste any more time or energy

Thinking about it _______

Talking about it _______

Using it as a crutch _______

Keeping me from being who I should be _______

Keeping me away from others _______

Losing sleep over something I can't change _______

Letting it make me feel insecure _______

Making me question my every move _______

Keeping my heart safe from hurt _______

Wow, another tough question-one I think we've all had to learn through life. There is much I had to understand in order to move ahead with my life, so I'm just as guilty of staying in the pain of things as everyone else.

85-Since that was so tough, let's take a break. Do you ever want to just be absolutely silly in life? Have you thought about some things and just never really pushed yourself to do them? For me, there are so many things to laugh at. My shopping excursions for example are fun moments to be a total idiot! It's way more fun with friends or family along at the time. I have made my nephews skip with me into a department store or I sing off key when they are close by so people can hear me. Ya know that's just darn right fun to hear that "Aunty would you stop!" –they're laughing though!

Have you ever done any of the following just to have fun with it all?

Embarrass someone while shopping in a fun way ____yes ____no

Sing loud enough for someone to look at you twice ____yes ____no

Play practical jokes (rubber snakes in the bed stuff) ____yes ____no

Belch loud and blame the other person ____yes ____no

Use playground equipment just for fun ____yes ____no

Make jokes while waiting in line somewhere ____yes ____no

Get all flirty with a shy single person in public ____yes ____no

86-Oh those little moments when you get to say "Gotcha" make it all worthwhile. It's just those naturally dorky things I do without thinking. Things that just make you stop and giggle. I've tripped, spilled food, dribbled, fallen up stairs, had the stomach noises in dead silence…yep, I'm classy at times but luckily the people with me had a sense of humor as well. I've watched people who tuck their skirts into their pantyhose, men with the shirt tail out the zipper of their pants-it's endless really.

Let's think of some of your moments when something just doesn't go right and it ends up being the fun moment of the evening for others. Spill it, what have ya done? Top 3 please:

1____

2____

3____

87-Yep, feels like that big spotlight is suddenly shining on you and we all have those moments-some at work, some in a crowd. It really is another thing we all share in common. It's usually when I first meet someone, perhaps a nervous reaction. Once, this rather attractive man came up to start a conversation and being attentive to his every word, I reached for my drink to take a sip and the straw was ever so attractively shoved up my nose. (You're laughing I can hear you from here). Another time I was at a work function and it was a beer which suddenly began foaming rapidly as I took my sip (Yep) I spewed it on the poor man's suit. Is it any wonder I'm single?

So, let's hear about 3 of your worst 'one on one' moments:

1____

____

2____

____

3____

____

88-We experience so much in life and I believe it is all in how you look at it. Even during those tough moments, someone usually comes along to make us laugh. Whether induced by a friend, co-worker or family member…at times, it's those very people who manage to make us see the light.

Who are the friends who always seem to make you laugh at life:

__________________ __________________ __________________

Who are the family members who help you giggle about the troubles:

__________________ __________________ __________________

At times, it is even the memory of someone we no longer have that helps us through. For me, it's my Dad. When life takes a crazy left turn, I think about what he would have said about it all. He still makes me laugh, feel stronger and helps me find my way at times. Is there anyone you still feel that connection with like they're looking out for you and laughing right beside you?

__________________ __________________ __________________

89-So, I hope by now you're looking at things from all different angles and you're choosing to move forward on your best foot. Isn't that what they say 'put your best foot forward'-so what is going to be your best foot?

I am planning in the next week to:

Go out and do something new & different ____yes ____no

Spend more time with friend's ____yes ____no

Spend quality time with family ____yes ____no

Do something fun with your children ____yes ____no

See yourself through new eyes ____yes ____no

Be open to support from others ____yes ____no

Face the days with a smile ____yes ____no

Smile more and strike up conversations with people ____yes ____no

Treat yourself to ____

Do you have your own ideals of what your best foot will be?

____

____

____

90-Wow, only 10 more to go and you're done this crazy book. I always try to get you to look ahead in the last few questions.
Seems we all go through rough spots and it's the one way we are all the same. No one ever has it easy in life, love, relationship, friendship…seems we all go through things; we just sometimes forget to listen or share those experiences. It's hard to look at our way of thinking at the moment and to simply reflect on the big picture. Emotions at times get in the way and it's good to get them out, but there comes the time when we choose to move forward with our new way of thinking and seeing things. I've done it, you've done it-every human being has done it. The hurts never are easy, but it is the coming to terms and letting it go that finally give us some peace.

So, thinking on that line, we will for the last time re-visit what you're feeling at this moment. You've had some time to think about everything so let's re-ask these questions to see if there are any changes in your answers:

What is the one thing you are most angry about-is it still there?

____

What is the hardest thing for you to accept, or do you have a better feeling about it all now?

___

What is the one thing you would like to say to the person who hurt you-or have you just accepted it is how it was meant to be?

___

What is your biggest fear about it all-or are you ready to be positive and push yourself forward?

___

What have you learned about yourself from this all-are you enlightened and proud of yourself?

___

What one trait will you make sure to watch for next time-maybe you won't watch need to watch as you are more confident in yourself now?

___

91-It would be nice to always get the answers to that illusive question–why-but at times there are no words. People change, expectations change, circumstances change, tragedies…we can't help things that happen sometimes. The only thing we ever have is to be the best we can be all the time. My motto will always be 'the amount I hurt in life is testimony to my capability of loving in life'. It is something I try to remember every day, especially in those hard moments.
What will be your new motto

___

92-It's easy to become skeptical in this life and yet, if we allow the hurts to change us we just may miss out on something wonderful. We all get scared to open our hearts don't we? After all we go through we may not be willing to give anyone the chance. It's the easiest way out, isn't it? To keeps us safe and unharmed, yet lonely. And when you lose your partner to illness or accident, it is heart wrenching.

In your own words, please write what you feel about your future and how you think you will view new people wanting to get close to you:

____

Now whatever you decide about the future it has an effect on everyone around you. Never thought of it that way maybe, but if we shut down all those who try to care for us, they in turn stop approaching others as they feel it's not worth the effort.

93-Is this world becoming one of no real contact? Things have become so easy to brush off, delete, pass over and pass by. It has become easier to just remain guarded and skeptical than reach out and try communicating differently. You certainly must see some things in this world that make you shake your head asking, why has it become this way? In your opinion, rate the following in order of what you think are the reasons for the way things are today-1 being the main reason, 10 being don't think it makes a difference in the big picture really and everything in between:

Not sharing time with others _______

Too much time alone _______

Afraid to talk openly _______

Scared to be vulnerable _______

Worried about self only _______

Lack of understanding _______

Lack of caring about others _______

Focused on work and achievement _______

Technology-Internet, texts _______

Insecurity _______

Been hurt too many times _______

Selling themself short _______

Expect too much from everyone _______

High maintenance personalities _______

Vanity _______

Advertising in society _______

Giving up on hope _______

Settling too soon _______

Afraid to change _______

Do you have some of your own to add?

____

____

____

We can change all these if we all try a little harder-is it possible?

94-We have the opportunity to interact everyday-the grocery clerk who rings you through, the neighbor who you see across the street, that person you pass every day on the way to work. There are opportunities everywhere for connecting with people. Even if they aren't what we would want in a partner, perhaps they have something in common as a friend. Now, I'm not saying befriend everyone you meet, but I'm saying what if we opened the door of communication more?

We are all simply people getting by every day with thoughts, habits, dreams, hurts and hopes. Who knows what new people may offer in life? If nothing else you've made their day by being the person who took the time for them.

Can you see yourself doing any of the following

Striking up conversation with new people ____yes ____no

Making the effort to approach others in daily life ____yes ____no

Taking a moment to listen to what they are about ____yes ____no

Listening to opinions more carefully _____yes ____no

Reaching out with a more positive outlook _____yes ____no

Telling friends/family how you really feel about them _____yes ____no

Sharing more of who you are with people _____yes ____no

Talking about the hard moments ____yes _____no

Understanding their life circumstances ____yes _____no

Asking how others are doing with things ____yes _____no

Usually in life it is the little things that can make the biggest difference. It is a fast paced society-we work hard, play hard and we get so busy we forget at times to take that extra moment to simply be more kind. We're in a hurry, we want what we want…what do you see when you stop and look at it all? We can make a difference every day for self and others…let's start working on it.

95-If nothing else, know you are not alone right now. There are thousands of people who are right where you are, hurt, struggling, trying to figure it all out and going through the tough moments.
There are no right words to make it better-no amount of ice cream and junk food will make it any easier (although they do taste yummy). You are exactly where you need to be. Now, that doesn't mean it can't and won't change or work out…it means you have a moment to look at who you are, where you want to go and what you want to do with your life.

You can't change anyone but yourself-ever. So looking at the next month, you honestly want to change what top 3 things?

1___________________________________

2___________________________________

3___________________________________

96-Sucks that we can't change anyone else, I know if I had a magic wand…nope-I wouldn't change a thing. Life is the unknown and it would be scary if we could see in the future. Gotta wing it! Doesn't mean we can't plan for and hope. So if you had that crystal ball for one moment, picture your life 1 year from now what do you see in your future?

What 3 things are you going to spend money on just for you

________________ ________________ ________________

What 3 things are you going to try doing just for fun

________________ ________________ ________________

What 3 new positive sayings are you going to follow in life

____

____

____

97-That's not bad 9 new things in 1 year and all do-able, you just have to believe in yourself. And you should just look at all you have in life. You're smart, funny (fill in 6 more)

________________ ________________ ________________

________________ ________________ ________________

98-That feels good doesn't it, knowing who we are inside and out. It's not always easy to see our way out of a situation. We get lost, life takes that left turn or we lose someone. Every person we ever meet teaches us something new, either how to love differently, enjoy different things, even silly things like how to cook or clean.

I guess it is truly on how we wish to view it all. So looking at this past speed bump you just went over…answer the following:

I truly believe that I have learned that the best thing about me is:

____

99-Two more and you're done…WHEW! What a lot of thinking you've done! You've had people who were concerned about you while you sorted through all this stuff…they've watched you going through the rough spot all along. If you could pass on the one most important thing about going through all this to your friends and family, you'd like to tell them that:

____

____

100-Wow! You made it! This one should come easy-you've had time to really look at your life and what you feel, even who you are. You are everything you were ever meant to be. You were brought into this world with special talents, attributes, characteristics, looks, thoughts, ways…you are unique, individual and special in this world. A person is truly measured by the sum total of who they are, not what they have or what they think the world expects them to be, look like or succeed in…on a scale from 1-10 (10 being perfect, 1-need to work on it a bit)

You'd say you are overall a ________

You would rate yourself on each of the following as:

Strength __________
Courage __________
Determination __________
Lovable __________
Understanding __________
Honest __________

No matter where we go in life, we affect someone else just as many times as we are affected. We don't always remember what our actions can really do. At times complete strangers get our moods or anger for no reason. Too often we forget to stop and think about that in the big picture. We have the ability to turn things around, shoot for the stars, give all we have and make life better for ourselves, those we love and those we come in contact with every day.

You've seen it and experienced it-a positive outlook can change a person and a whole room just as much as a negative one can. I know you'll find your way through to the next phase of your life, feel secure in knowing that everything turns out as it should…just move forward thinking about all you have to offer this world. I do hope this has helped somewhat. Nothing is ever easy or simple and at times we just have to go through the motions. Smile! I believe you're onto greater things in life!

Wendy Proteau

Blessed with three siblings and parents who supported my hopes, I was raised in a small Canadian town, in an average middle-class family. Single at age forty-something, I'm still figuring life out daily. Being a combination of realist and dreamer, you can only imagine the confusion that goes on internally. Half of me writes a story with 'the happily ever after', the other half, edits the work and keeps it more realistic.

I'd never written more than a grocery list until 2009. It came out of nowhere as I sat at my computer following an idea. The '*Sit N Do Nothing Hamster Series'* is my way to bring us all a little closer in this technological world. The workbooks of self-discovery are a way to share tidbits of who we are, in the here and now. Each of the seven volumes, designed for a specific audience, asks the reader about their lives. I have many more ideas to expand the series. This hamster never quits! They are now available via print on demand.

Finding my inner voice, I decided to try my hand at a fiction. *'And When'* was written from September 2010–January 2011. Receiving many reviews, the story resonated, often bringing them to tears, laughter, and at times… needing a cold towel.

Taking months to edit the final draft, I began to miss that creative energy and '*Now What'* the sequel was started in 2012 and published in 2013. The story continues to place difficult hurdles, forcing the characters to veer from their chosen paths.

My life would be nothing without the people who have touched my soul. Friends, family, co-workers, relatives…have all been there through the good and bad. Everything takes hard work and nothing ever comes easy. Well at least not in my life. I firmly believe that karma plays an important role. It brings us the people we are meant to meet, challenges we have to overcome, lessons we need to learn and dreams we are meant to reach for.

The Sit 'N' Do Nothing Hamster Series

Unlock Your Hamster-Volume One
An introduction to the series

The Single Man Hamster-Volume Two

The Single Woman Hamster-Volume Three

Hamsters Unite-The Relationship-Volume Four
Dating, Married or Living Together

Heart Broke Hamster-Volume Five
For the tough spots of break-up, divorce or loss

The Gotta Have Hamster-Volume Six
Advertising and what you buy into

The Hospital Hamster-Volume Seven
For those in hospital or home recuperating

www.ingramcontent.com/pod-product-compliance
Lightning Source LLC
Chambersburg PA
CBHW080528030426
42337CB00023B/4664

* 9 7 8 0 9 8 6 8 9 8 7 4 7 *